START INVESTING NOW:

Making Your Money Work for You

A Beginner's Guide to the Stock Market and Planning a Successful Financial Future

P.W. KING

© **Copyright 2021 - All rights reserved.**

The content contained within this book may not be reproduced, duplicated, or transmitted without direct written permission from the author or the publisher.

Under no circumstances will any blame or legal responsibility be held against the publisher, or author, for any damages, reparation, or monetary loss due to the information contained within this book, either directly or indirectly.

Legal Notice:

This book is copyright protected. It is only for personal use. You cannot amend, distribute, sell, use, quote or paraphrase any part, or the content within this book, without the consent of the author or publisher.

Disclaimer Notice:

Please note the information contained within this document is for educational and entertainment purposes only. All effort has been executed to present accurate, up to date, reliable, complete information. No warranties of any kind are declared or implied. Readers acknowledge that the author is not engaged in the rendering of legal, financial, medical, or professional advice. The content within this book has been derived from various sources. Please consult a licensed professional before attempting any techniques outlined in this book.

By reading this document, the reader agrees that under no circumstances is the author responsible for any losses, direct or indirect, that are incurred as a result of the use of the information contained within this document, including, but not limited to, errors, omissions, or inaccuracies.

Special Bonus!

Want this Bonus Book for Free?

Get **FREE**, unlimited access to it and to all of my new books by joining the Fan Base!

SCAN WITH YOUR CAMERA **TO JOIN!**

Table of Contents

Introduction 9
    Getting an Early Start 10
    Fear Is Unjustified 11
Chapter 1: Why Start Now? 13
    The Time Value of Money 15
    Habits for the Future 18
Chapter 2: The Reasons You're Not Investing 21
    Personal Finance 23
    Finding the Cash 26
Chapter 3: What Is the Stock Market? 30
    Basic Laws 34
    Trading Versus Investing 36
Chapter 4: Let's Get Started! 39
    Finding a Broker 43
    Setting Things up 47
Chapter 5: Goals, Strategies, and Account Types 50
    Types of Accounts 51
    Cash Versus Margin 55
Chapter 6: What to Buy 59
    Your Options 61
    Diversification Examples 69

Chapter 7: Things to Avoid 77
    Common Errors 78
    What Makes a Good Investor? 81
Chapter 8: This Is Just the Beginning 84
    Cryptocurrency, Forex, and Commodities Trading
    89
    Direct Real Estate Investing 94
Conclusion 100
    In Practice 102
    It Starts Yesterday 104
References 107

Introduction

The world of finance and investing seems daunting to many of us. On the news, we see figures and arrows representing the current market performance or the price of gold. Now and then, we catch stories of downturns in an industry, poor forecasts for the market, and big-name companies that have lost stock value. To an outsider, this can give the impression that the stock market is a place filled with risk and uncertainty. Some cunning experts make their millions, while others lose everything in a day.

Scarier than the stock market is a little thing called inflation. You have probably grown tired of hearing your grandparents talk about how everything cost a dime back in the day. Behind those stories is a reality that the cost of living rises every year, reducing the value of money that is not earning interest. Inflation is also combined with the bittersweet knowledge that people are living longer and will continue to live longer, ever-increasing the length of retirement.

Recent research published by the Morning Consult (2019) revealed that 50% of Americans aged between 18 and 34 are not investing towards their retirement. Part of the reason is that people are not sure how. Another factor is that they think that retirement is just a distant thought, that it isn't important. Some have convinced themselves that they will start when they are older and have more money. This can cause a compounding problem. When you get older, you have more expenses, such as children and mortgages. These obligations cost a great deal more than the expenses of socializing and enjoying your youth. The truth is that investing is easier than you think, but it will not get easier with age.

The best way to process the fact that 50% of young people do not invest is to think about the other half. Who are they? They are regular people like you and me. They represent the whole of America's working world. They work in every occupation imaginable, but they all have one thing in common. They are investors, and if they are doing it, anyone can. These people are proof that gaining sound knowledge of the markets and investing is within the grasp of all of us. It is not necessary to have a degree in finance or have friends on Wall Street. The first step in the process is to start at the beginning with an open mind. Once you have read this book, you will be equipped with the basic tools to start investing and to dramatically alter your financial future. In fact, you are likely to look back and wonder why you ever avoided investing in the first place!

Getting an Early Start

Investing at a young age is not simply a marketing ploy, created by finance companies to scare you into giving them your money. The benefits of developing investment habits as early as possible are real and very powerful. A basic example would be the difference between a person investing at age 25 and age 30. If we were to assume a retirement age of 65 years and an average return on investment of 8% per year, a 25-year-old would need to contribute 486.97 dollars per month to retire with 1.7 million dollars. If the same person started at age 30, they would need to invest 741.10 dollars in order to achieve the same result.

A teenager might think that they don't have that kind of money, but if the same person in the above example saved just 50 dollars per month from age 18 to 25, they would add an extra 118,000 dollars to their retirement savings at age 65. It becomes quite disappointing to consider that, as recently as four years ago, surveys conducted with retirees found that over 53% of respondents had saved just 25,000 dollars, with as many as one-third of retirees saving a mere 1,000 dollars. To put that into perspective, a person saving just 50 dollars per month from age 25 at an average return of 8% would have just over 109,000 dollars at retirement. Far too many people sell themselves short by not realizing the value of investing and have to rely on social security at a time in their lives when they should be enjoying the freedom of retirement.

Fear Is Unjustified

The Standard and Poor's 500 index (S&P 500) is a measure of the performance and average return of the top 500 companies in the US stock market. It is considered to be an accurate reflection of the performance of the stock market as a whole. The average returns of the S&P 500 over the last forty years are approximately 12%. The average return for the stock market over the last century is roughly 10%. Naturally, the performance of the stock market can rise and dip over a period of a year or even five years. However, investing is a long-term game, and the performance of the market over time demonstrates that the total performance of stocks has grown and will continue to grow. The simple key to the market is to accept that short-term dips may occur, but over the period of your working life, the market will produce positive returns that comfortably exceed your real enemy, inflation. The long-term average inflation rate over the last century has been 3.1%. As with the market, over shorter terms, the inflation rate has been higher or lower, but it will be a constant threat to your money all the time.

The good news is that the market, despite its ups and downs, has beaten your real fear easily and consistently. Time can either work for you, or it can work against you. The market is far more reliable than many people give it credit for, and it will be the ideal vehicle for your financial dreams and security. You will learn through reading this book that investing can be fun, but most importantly, it is empowering. Once your eyes have been opened to the simple methods of growing your wealth, you will be capable of guiding your own financial future. Time is of the essence; do not miss out on valuable years of wealth creation. Grab the opportunity with both hands and enjoy becoming the boss of your own money!

Chapter 1: Why Start Now?

Avoiding the need to invest is like avoiding your household chores. You can tell yourself that you will clean the refrigerator tomorrow or you will mow the lawn next week. Somehow, something always comes up, and days become weeks, and sometimes months. The job of cleaning your refrigerator becomes tougher, and cutting the grass takes more time and effort. When the problem has become so bad that you must confront it, you always end up having to pay a higher price in time, effort, and personal sacrifice. Starting young lets you put aside less and allows time to work its magic for you.

Another great reason to start now would be to look at the books that are written for people in their 50s who are only just starting to invest for retirement. I can save you time: The common advice is to get a second job and to consider postponing retirement. Unfortunately, people do not have the option of telling their younger selves to make changes. Not being ready for retirement places a burden upon you, and it can also affect your children if they have to support you in your old age.

When people invest at a younger age, it also enables them to expand their goals to include other expenses apart from retirement. Your biggest purchase in life will most likely be your home. When you are young and do not need to sacrifice as much for your retirement plans, you can also invest towards a deposit on your first house or flat. With youth comes options.

Saving and investing are considered to be the same thing. However, in reality, they are not. Saving is typically short term, and what banks call "savings accounts" will pay you an interest rate that is lower than inflation. Remember that, if you are not beating inflation, you are losing money. Putting money in a bank savings account is not much better than putting money under your mattress or in a cookie jar. Investment is long term, and it's about building wealth and financial security.

One of the more inspiring investment stories of recent years is that of Ronald Read. Read spent his life working at a gas station and as a janitor. From a young age, he got into the habit of investing in stocks, eventually owning stock in more than one hundred companies. Throughout his life, he lived through many ups and downs on the market. There was the Kennedy slide of 1962, Black Monday in 87, and the dot-com bubble of 2000. At the time of his death in 2014, Read had acquired a fortune of 8 million dollars. This had been achieved on a modest income, but with time and diligence, he did it.

Financial analysts have looked at Read's accomplishments to see if he was lucky or whether others could replicate his performance. Read began investing in 1948 in his mid-twenties with about 50 dollars per month. Adjusted for inflation, that would be about 530 dollars today. It was concluded that

Americans today could match his earnings if they invested 530 dollars a month and increased the amount in line with inflation every year. This is a manageable amount for many households, but even if 500 dollars is currently above your means, it should demonstrate what an average person can do with time and an investment habit.

The Time Value of Money

The concept of the time value of money centers around the idea that money in your hand now is worth more than the same amount at a later stage. This is because money has earning potential. The ability to earn compound interest is what provides the growth potential for your money. The power of compound interest is often overlooked, but it is a wonderful thing. Earning interest upon interest is what creates exponential growth over time.

For example, if you were to invest 5,000 dollars at an interest rate of 10% for 5 years, you would have over 8,000 dollars. If you were to leave that money for another 5 years, you would have almost 13,000 dollars. You earned an extra 3,000 dollars in your first five years, but over the next five years, you earned an extra 5,000 dollars. As every extra five-year period goes by, your earnings will become greater and greater. If you invested this sum for 25 years, your last 5 years would earn you an extra 17,000 dollars.

Another eye-opening contrast is between a savings account and the stock market. The best interest rate on a bank savings account in the US is currently 0.57%. If you left 5,000 dollars in that account for 5 years, you would have the sum of 5,144 dollars. Compared with the historical return of the market of 10%, the difference is substantial. It is also important to understand that inflation is the opposite of compound interest. If we assume that inflation is 2.5%, and you were to leave your 5,000 dollars under your bed for 5 years, it would have the purchasing power of 4,400 dollars. Within 28 years, your money would halve in value.

When you are comparing the return or average interest rate between different investments, it is important for you to understand the distinction between the nominal and effective interest rate. This can lead to errors in comparison between your investment options. Generally, banks and investment firms will post the annual returns of a fund or asset using the nominal annual rate. However, the nominal return is a simple annual average. For example, some assets and funds will pay interest on a quarterly basis. If you are paid two percent interest for four quarters, then your nominal return is presented as eight percent. This is not the effective rate, or *yield* as it is called. If you are paid interest on a quarterly basis and the interest is reinvested, then over the span of a year, the actual return that you receive will be a bit higher than eight percent. The nominal return would only be accurate if you received interest payments once a year. As soon as you are paid more than once per year, then the compounding effect is greater, and you are getting interest upon your quarterly interest. A practical example can illustrate the point with a one-hundred-dollar amount. If you earned eight percent interest, paid once per year, you would have 108 dollars. If you earned eight percent interest but paid quarterly at a rate of two percent per quarter, then you would have 108.24 dollars at the end. That would be your effective return, or yield. It may not seem like a big difference, but over many years of compounding, it can result in a large difference.

When looking at funds, stocks, and other investments, in order to ensure that you are comparing returns properly, it is good to know if your interest payments are paid more than once per year. Also, confirm if the projected returns or past performance of the asset are posted as nominal or effective rates. Another way to assess the performance of an investment is to calculate the real return. This is done by deducting the average inflation rate from the average return. For example, if an investment has had an average return of eight percent, but inflation has averaged two percent over the same time, your real return is six percent. It is important to think in these terms because the compounding of inflation will have an impact over the course of an investment. Future sums of money are not worth the same as present sums. This will be essential to you in the next chapter when you start to think about your investment goals, both retirement and otherwise. When you think of how much money you would need to be comfortable in old age, the current amount would need to take inflation into account. That inflation-adjusted amount would be your real investment goal.

Habits for the Future

You start to form your natural ingrained habits when you are young. Many basic temperaments and tendencies will already be formed in your childhood. However, your attitude to money and how you spend it will, to a large extent, be formed when you first enter the working world. Habits, both good and bad, can take many months to form. The spending and financial habits that you develop over the early years of your working life will shape the decades to come.

Spending more than you earn or never saving for years will become a habit in itself. Once this habit and mindset have gained a foothold in your month-to-month life, you will find that it gets hard to snap out of it. The longer the habit remains, the harder it will be to conquer it. Developing a good habit comes about in the same way as the harmful ones do. It is created by a series of little actions and choices that eventually become patterns and ultimately a way of being. The little habit-forming action of investing is to set aside money every month. These amounts can be small, but if you make it a routine, it can develop into a habit. Investing is a lot like exercising. One workout does not seem to make much difference. A five-minute workout can seem meaningless. It can be discouraging when you first start to see people running ten miles or hitting the gym bike for an hour. Other people seem so far ahead of you that you will never catch up. Any good fitness coach will tell you that how much you exercise or how hard you work out is not what is most important. If you want to be healthy and reasonably fit, then your top priority is to simply develop a routine. Everything else stems from that basic foundation. If you can only handle five minutes, four times a week, that is fine. As long as it becomes a routine that you stick to, you will progress over time.

The investing habit is the same. You can start very small, but if the routine is there, the habit will follow, and so will the progress. The one difference between fitness and investing is that your fitness has a definite limit. With the power of compound interest, your little contributions will grow over time and develop into wealth. Investing is only limited by time.

Good habits breed other good habits. Being in charge of your finances and using the knowledge in this book will motivate you and empower you to make better choices in other areas of your life, from choosing your first home to purchase to deciding what financial goals really matter to you. Investing and practicing good personal planning will bring financial freedom and open your eyes to options that you may never have thought of. Little by little, the molehill will grow into a mountain. Habit and knowledge are all you need. The following chapters will progressively build your understanding of the market and investing. You will come to realize that wealth creation is not so complicated. In fact, you will wish you had started yesterday.

Chapter 2: The Reasons You're Not Investing

The fear of the stock market and investment world is one reason why people avoid thinking about their retirement. There are many other reasons though, particularly with young people. When you are young, your priorities are different. There are many pearls of wisdom, such as "enjoy your youth while you have it," which can create imbalances in your spending habits and create the impression that you have plenty of time. You may tell yourself you will invest when you earn more money or when you have paid your debts.

Wanting to time the market is another pitfall to avoid. Telling yourself that you will invest when the market improves can be an illusion. To begin with, investment professionals will tell you that timing the market is extremely difficult, and many fail to do so. Good research over the years has also shown that investors who attempt to time markets do not get better returns compared with investors who stuck it out over the same period. Even if the market is not performing at all-time highs, you will still be earning more interest than if you put your money in a piggy bank or you simply did not save at all.

A lot of people start to take retirement more seriously beyond age thirty, when they have kids and a mortgage to pay. Interestingly, this is also when people start to vote and to take their futures more seriously in general. It is a paradox that people become wearier of their long-term prospects at a time when their obligations and financial burdens become greater. You may be making more money at this stage of your life, but your essential expenses have also increased.

You might also think that, because you can only invest a small amount, it is not worth it, or you don't know how much you should invest. When you are older, you are forced to go through a process where you determine the difference between your wants and your needs. The act of having your first child almost always requires a change in spending habits because you have another person to pay for. These life milestones result in people coming to grips with how they spend, and sometimes waste, their money. Often, the basic principle of paying yourself first is misunderstood.

The concept of paying yourself first is simple but very important. Surveys of the common traits of wealthy people will always hone in on the fact that they have a pay-yourself-first mindset. It is the same kind of thinking that successful investors need to have. This does not mean that you treat yourself to your every desire. It is about putting money aside for your long-term goals before you have spent a cent on anything else. Investing for your future before you spend on your current wants or nice-to-haves is what paying yourself first is really all about. This involves working out how much you can invest on a monthly basis and sticking to it. The easiest way to do this is to have a monthly electronic transfer on your bank account that transfers your money directly into a retirement account, either through work or through an IRA.

The first step is to commit now to the process of reviewing your personal finances. You have heard it many times before, but it is a basic truth. When people take a serious look at what they actually spend their money on, there will generally be many areas where they spend unnecessarily. Finding money, even small amounts, is not as hard as you may think. We have already demonstrated the power of compound interest and the benefit of starting the investment habit early. All you need to do now is find those small amounts and get busy creating wealth.

Personal Finance

Paying yourself first and getting your personal finances in order is not about sacrificing your quality of life. You are not going to be advised to live on bread and cheese in order to hoard your money. The trick is to cut out wasteful expenses that we can all be guilty of. Conduct a personal lifestyle audit, and identify your essential costs, genuine quality-of-life expenses, and all of the other things that you spend money on without much thought.

A habit to get into is to assess your total financial situation every year. As time goes by, you may earn more money, or your essential expenses will increase. Assessing your finances once a year is not time-consuming, and it's important for knowing what your priorities are for the year ahead. Commence by calculating your expected income for the year. If you have the kind of job where it may be hard to know what your earnings will be, then give yourself a conservative estimate.

Next, you should determine what your basic household expenses will be and any other unavoidable costs. If you have debt, work out how much and how long you will need to pay. Debt for some of us cannot be avoided, but it is a good practice to keep it as low as possible. This is where short-term saving can be valuable. Store credit and loans are very expensive, and if you can pay for something by saving a little for a few months, it's far better and cheaper than racking up debt.

Once you know what your unavoidable and basic costs are, you can subtract them from your expected earnings. The result will show you what you have left for investment and quality of life. Deduct your known expenses for hobbies and activities to see what is left. If you still have money left over, this will give you a good idea of how much money you spend on unimportant things.

Another common error made by a lot of people is paying too much tax. This is because they are not fully aware of what expenses are tax-deductible. For example, a portion of your student loan, the interest on your mortgage, and medical expenses are deductible. Students, in particular, should be aware that the interest on all loans for higher education, not just federal loans, are deductible up to a maximum of 2500 dollars per year. Even if you pay only 12% tax on a modest income, that is a 300-dollar refund.

These are already sources of money that you could save and could put towards investing. You may need to visit a tax consultant to fully understand all of your possible deductions, but one visit is all it takes, which will not be expensive. Remember that avoiding paying too much tax is not evading tax; you are simply giving your own money away unnecessarily. Getting tax deductions also requires record keeping. Some people are aware of what they can claim, but they do not bother to keep receipts and accounts for things like medical costs, which bites them when it comes time to file tax returns.

At this stage of the process, you are now ready to set your investment goal. The money that you have may not be as much as you would like, but molehills become mountains with time and compound interest. When you pay yourself first, you will know how much that needs to be. Follow the below steps to get a better idea of how much you can invest.

- ❏ Assess your financial situation
- ❏ Calculate your expected income
- ❏ Determine your household expenses
- ❏ Determine your debt
- ❏ Minimize your tax
- ❏ Identify wasteful expenditure
- ❏ Set your investment goal

Common advice for investors is to pay off all debt first. This can put you in a situation where you neglect your investment goal for too long. Long-term debt, such as student loans and mortgages, cannot be avoided, but using them as a reason for not investing would delay your investment goal for years or even indefinitely. It is best to do both at the same time, using your tax deduction to supplement your investment goal. As time goes by and you have extra cash on occasion, it could be better to invest rather than pay off debt faster. It would depend on your debt interest rate. For example, if your student loan or mortgage interest rate is 5% and a conservative return on your investment is 7%, it would make sense to invest with spare cash.

Finding the Cash

You may be like many people after going through the personal finance process, who conclude that they just don't have any spare money. Don't be too hard on yourself, because there are a few things that you can consider. Unless you are someone that lives on the poverty line, there will be ways that you might not have thought of to free up money for investing. We will run through some simple ways to save money that can actually add up to a reasonable sum.

Go through your food bill. Separate how much money you spend on household food and how much you spend on eating out. Do you throw a lot of food away each month? If so, you can reduce the amount of those foods that you buy. If you throw away a lot of food because you end up eating out all of the time, then this is perhaps an area that you should focus on. When looking at how much you eat out, ask yourself if it is necessary and if you could eat at cheaper places more often. Young people, in particular, are not big on home cooking, but it is an obvious area where you could tighten your belt. If you are inclined to buy lunch every day at work, then perhaps making your own lunch half of the days will save you quite a bit over a month.

If you have a mortgage, consider having it refinanced. The interest rates may have come down for current loans, and you are missing an opportunity. Provided that you have had your current mortgage for twelve months or longer and you have 10% home equity, you could apply for refinancing. Saving just one percent interest on your loan can reduce your monthly payment and save money over the duration of your mortgage. If you do not qualify for refinancing and you took your mortgage without paying a deposit, you will be paying mortgage insurance. If you have paid off 20% of your loan so far, you can ask your mortgage firm to stop the insurance payments, which will reduce your monthly cost.

Take a look at your cell phone bill. The average American spends just under 100 dollars a month on their cell phone. You can explore the option of getting a phone through a prepaid wireless provider that will bring your bill down. You could well be paying for talk time, messages, or data that you don't really use. Choose the prepaid option that suits your usage needs, and you will certainly save, particularly if you are the average person currently spending 100 dollars.

Depending on your age, you may have cable TV. The average American household is spending around 200 dollars per month on cable. These days, there are many streaming services that offer all of the same content and sports for a fraction of the price. You could easily save yourself 100 dollars per month.

If you aren't already, start paying your bills online. Depending on how many bills you have, sending checks in the mail will cost you quite a lot more. By paying online, you could be saving anything from 50 to 85 dollars per year.

Consider paying with cash for your day-to-day purchases. Psychologically, it's easier to keep track of what you spend. Swiping cards is so quick, but often you will only realize how much you were spending at the end of the month.

The task of finding savings in your personal life may be easy for some, harder for others. By minimizing your tax, reducing unnecessary expenditure, and perhaps with a little restraint, you will be able to start your investment journey. We have already learned how an amount of just 50 dollars per month is a meaningful amount that will grow to a surprising figure over time. Your only challenge is to commit and create an entrenched habit that will serve you well as the years roll by. In time, you can invest more. For the moment, it is more important to create the habit of reviewing your financial status on a regular basis, having a goal, and being in charge of your personal finances. Only good things can come from this.

Chapter 3: What Is the Stock Market?

Exchanges appeared in their earliest forms in Europe towards the end of the twelfth century. In most cases, they were literally markets in a town square where commodities such as wheat and vegetables were traded. Banks also traded early forms of government bonds at these markets, and debt was also traded between lenders. The capital market as we know it today had not fully formed yet. The Dutch East India Company was the first enterprise in history to issue publicly traded stocks in the 1600s. This paved the way for what we know today as modern stock exchanges.

New York launched its stock exchange (NYSE) in 1792. Philadelphia officially launched the first exchange in America, but the New York exchange quickly became the largest. For about two centuries, the NYSE had little competition from other smaller exchanges in the US. However, in 1971, the NASDAQ was launched. NASDAQ is not a physical market, but a virtual one. It is a fully computerized global securities exchange where some of the largest companies in the world are listed.

Company stock is often called *equity*, and it represents the stockholders' ownership in the company. You may have heard news stories about a company going "public" or choosing to list on the stock exchange.

Companies do this in order to raise funds. It may be to expand the business or to invest more in research and product development. Either way, when a company issues stock, it is effectively borrowing money from the investors that purchase the stock. When you own stocks or an individual stock in a company, you own a small portion of that company, and in principle, you have voting rights at their annual shareholders' meeting. In exchange for purchasing stock, the company is obligated to give you a share of the profits, which is called a *dividend payment*. This is really no different from being a money lender that charges interest. The dividend payment is your interest for the money that has been lent. The total return of your stock over any period of time would be the dividend payments combined with any growth in the value of the stock itself.

Stock markets are physical and virtual venues where buyers and sellers can meet to trade. Typically, as an investor, you would purchase stocks through a broker or an electronic trading platform, which are middlemen. They facilitate the exchange between buyer and seller and also assist with enforcing the exchange's rules regarding transparency. Prospective investors would make what is called a *bid* for a specific stock, which is simply an offer to purchase at a set price. Sellers of stock would have an *ask*, which is the price that they are prepared to sell at. When the bid and the ask are equal, a trade can be made. This is very much like an auction. Stock markets provide what are called *primary* and *secondary* markets. When companies are issuing stocks for the first time, which is called an *initial public offering* (IPO), the exchange serves as a primary market. When those same stocks are traded from one owner to another, the exchange is a secondary market.

The benefit of the stock market comes from what the financial world calls *liquidity*. This refers to the ease or speed at which you can buy and sell a stock for a price that is a fair reflection of its current value. By creating a large market, you are ensuring that there will always be a healthy number of both buyers and sellers to create what is known as *supply and demand*. The world of stocks is further divided by sectors. Over the last two centuries, some new sectors have developed. Currently, there are eleven sectors that describe the companies found on the exchange. These sectors include energy, healthcare, financials, real estate, information technology, and others.

The performance of individual sectors quite closely matches the performance of the American market over its total history, which is approximately a 10% average return. If you were to take a five-year slice out of the history of the market, you may find that the market has performed under 10%. Pick another five-year slice, and you will find that the market performed better than 10%. However, if you take a step back and you look at 35- to 40-year slices, you will find that the market grows at an average return of close to the historical 10%. Your retirement investing lifespan will be 40 years or longer if you start now! This is why investing is a long-term game, and over longer terms, the market is not as volatile as you may have previously thought.

The market continues to grow long term in spite of rises and dips because of increases in productivity, innovation, and technological progress. It could also be argued that population increases result in more economically productive people, which also expands the market. Arguably one of the world's greatest investors, Warren Buffet, had this to say about the economy:

"American GDP per capita is now about $56,000. In real terms – that's a staggering six times the amount in 1930, the year I was born, a leap far beyond the wildest dreams of my parents or their contemporaries. U.S. citizens are not intrinsically more intelligent today, nor do they work harder than did Americans in 1930. Rather, they work far more efficiently and thereby produce far more. This all-powerful trend is certain to continue."

While stock exchanges mainly facilitate the trading of equities, they are also venues for the trading of corporate bonds, exchange-traded funds (ETFs), REITs, or real estate investment trusts, and derivatives. These alternative investments will be explained in detail in Chapters 6 and 8.

Basic Laws

In the field of economics, there exist a few laws which explain the basics of how markets work and how individual stock prices are determined at any given time. The two fundamental concepts are scarcity and supply and demand. Scarcity is based on the fact that all goods and resources are limited; sometimes they are freely available, and sometimes there are shortages. When a good or resource becomes scarce, it will generally become more valuable, and its price will rise. For example, if you are the only plumber in Chicago, you could name your price. In some cases, the scarcity of one good may force the market to seek alternatives, raising the value and price of the alternative. If for some reason there was a shortage of butter, then people would have to pay more or purchase margarine instead. Scarcity, to a large extent, drives the law of supply and demand.

The law of demand states that, when prices are high, buyers will demand less. The law of supply states that, when prices are high, sellers will supply more. These two forces working together are what determine the final market price of a good or service and the total volume that will be sold. Using the plumber in Chicago as an example, the scarcity of his service creates high demand, which is what allows him to charge a high fee. However, if there were hundreds of other plumbers, the demand for his service would drop, and he would be forced to lower his fees. Another example could be that of peaches. The general demand for peaches is, say, 50,000 cases per month. If there were to be a disaster, such as a disease that affects peach trees, and many farmers suffer large reductions in the number of peaches that they can bring to market, this will cause a shortage of supply, or scarcity. Perhaps only 20,000 cases of peaches are available. This will drive up the price of peaches, and the buyers that want their share will have to compete by paying a higher price.

The laws of scarcity and supply and demand are alive and well on stock exchanges. They are what fuel the auction process between buyer and seller. The demand for a particular stock may be driven by a good history of dividend payments. The stock could be from a sector such as health care that is expected to grow rapidly over a period of time. The company in question may be revealing a new product range that is expected to sell very well and produce good profits. The owners of that stock may not be prepared to sell at the current market price, creating scarcity, or a shortage of supply. This would drive up the ask and the bid for that stock until a seller was prepared to accept a bid. The result of this process would be the new market price of the stock. Likewise, if a company has become less profitable over time, the demand for its stock will decline, and current stockholders may wish to sell. If the demand for the stock is lower than the supply, the bids will be lower than the asks. This will generally result in the seller having to accept a lower bid.

Trading Versus Investing

Both traders and investors seek to generate profits, but they go about it in different ways. Traders of stocks attempt to make small ongoing profits by trying to capitalize on stocks when the market is up and down. This involves daily, weekly, and monthly buying and selling. This practice costs more in terms of transaction fees and also carries more risk. Stocks are held for short periods and sold for a small profit. Naturally, this strategy requires a trader to "read" the market and movement of individual stocks on a daily basis, which requires full-time dedication and skill. Research has demonstrated that as little as one percent of traders make a great deal of money, while the rest will earn fairly modest monthly earnings. If traders are using other people's money, they could lose it and not earn any money at all. It is the practice of traders and their depiction in a number of movies that have probably given a lot of people their fear of the market and its perceived risks.

Investment, on the other hand, is defined by what is called a "buy-and-hold" strategy. It involves the purchase of valuable stocks and keeping them for long periods in order to earn dividends to reinvest and to gain growth in the value of the stocks. Remember that the market over time is quite consistent, and the ups and downs are "smoothed" out over the long term. An investor ignores the temporary fluctuations in prices and holds on for the long-run growth. Research conducted by the CFA institute that analyzed the investment habits of over a thousand people found that investors who behave like traders, buying and selling frequently, tend to make little to no returns over time. All the more reason to be a long-haul player.

A person can choose to be a direct investor or an indirect investor. In the case of direct investors, they will purchase stocks through a broker and will own their stocks directly. This also involves the investor choosing the stocks which they will buy and determining how they will reinvest the dividends themselves. This is not a scary option, but it does require an investor to develop more in-depth knowledge of the market and the companies whose stock they wish to invest in.

Indirect investment typically involves an investor giving their money to a firm that pools the money of many other investors and, in turn, buys stocks and securities on their behalf. The investor would own a "share" of the assets and stocks that are owned by the fund. This type of investment is common with workplace retirement funds. The benefit of indirect investment is that the investors' money is managed by professionals. It also allows people to invest in assets such as malls and offices, which they could not do on their own. Examples of indirect investment would be mutual funds and exchange-traded funds (ETFs).

Some of your fear of the stock market should be fading. The American exchange has been around for some two hundred years. It has grown over time, and it continues to grow. After reading this book, you will be fully informed and can decide if you would like to be a direct or indirect investor. The option of using professionals is available. Investing is not only essential for your financial future; it can also be fun to learn more about the market and how your wealth is made.

Chapter 4: **Let's Get Started!**

Traditional company pension plans that provide a set amount upon retirement are becoming increasingly rare these days. The most popular retirement investment vehicle offered by employers is the 401(k). It gets its name from the section of the internal revenue code that deals with retirement regulations. Company employees can make automatic payroll contributions on a monthly basis, which is ideal for paying yourself first. Many companies that offer 401(k) retirement options for their employees will also have a matching policy. This means that the company will contribute a certain amount to match the amount which the employee pays. Policies can vary from company to company, but typically, an employer will either match an employee's contribution dollar for dollar or will pay 50 cents for every dollar an employee contributes. The total amount that you can contribute will sometimes be capped at a percentage of your gross salary.

Apart from kicking off your personal wealth strategy, 401(k) accounts offer you a tax benefit. If you have the 401(k) option at work, you will be able to choose between what is called a traditional 401(k) and a Roth 401(k). Both types of 401(k) have tax benefits, but the nature of the benefits is different. With the traditional option, your contributions are tax-deductible in the year that they were made. During the lifespan of your investment, you would be able to use your tax refund to invest even more in a second investment account. However, upon retirement, your withdrawals from the 401(k) will become taxable. The amount that you are taxed will depend on your annual withdrawal. The traditional 401(k) is generally recommended for people who think that their retirement income will be less than their salary when they were working. This may be a good decision point, but it does neglect the benefit of being able to invest your annual tax deductions as well. The power of compound interest on your refunds will be substantial.

Contributions to a Roth 401(k) are not tax-deductible. The benefit kicks in at retirement. Unlike the traditional option, with a Roth, you will not be required to pay tax on your withdrawals. This is why the Roth option is generally recommended for people who feel that their retirement income will be greater than their salaries when they were working. The trade-off with the Roth is that you sacrifice your tax deduction during the term of your investment in exchange for tax-free withdrawals after retirement. Investors who favor the Roth 401(k) are of the opinion that paying no tax on your withdrawals results in more money in retirement. Again, they do not consider the option of investing your deduction as well.

Both the traditional and Roth 401(k)s allow you to access your money without penalties at age 59.5 unless you are permanently disabled. Accessing your money early will result in a 10% penalty over and above your taxes. The maximum contribution that a person under

50 can make to a 401(k) is 19,500 dollars as of 2021. An amount of 26,000 is allowed for workers over the age of 50. However, if your employer matches your contribution, then the maximum amount will increase. With an employer match, you can contribute 58,000 dollars per year and 64,000 dollars if you are over 50. The benefits of an employer match are tremendous, and if you have this option, you should contribute as much as you can in order to get the highest possible employer match. As a newcomer to investing, this should be your first goal. Your employer match is essentially free money to increase your wealth over time.

In the case of both 401(k)s, there are also minimum required withdrawals that are imposed beyond age 72. These minimum percentages are based upon calculated life expectancy. If by some chance you are still employed at this age, you may be exempt from the minimum withdrawals. It is possible to balance your contributions between both types of 401(k), but the total contributions must still be within the allowed limits. Most companies that offer 401(k)s will provide a choice of mutual funds from a single finance company and will have a standard option. It is important to know that, in many instances, you will have a choice and will not need to accept the standard fund. Your options of funds and the reasons behind them will be examined in detail in Chapters 5 and 6.

The 403(b) retirement plan is offered to government employees and people who work for tax-exempt institutions, such as not-for-profit organizations. The 403(b) is similar and different from the 401(k) that is offered to private-sector workers. Like with the 401(k), investors in 403(b)s have the choice of a traditional or Roth account for tax purposes. The minimum withdrawal ages are the same, and the maximum contributions are also the same. If you have an employer who offers both a 401(k) and the 403(b), then you could balance your money between both, but still within the contribution limit.

The 403(b) differs from the 401(k) in that the 403(b) does not need to comply with the Employee Retirement Income Security Act (ERISA). This can result in lower administrative fees; however, 403(b) plans that do not comply with ERISA are not allowed to have employer contributions, which can be a big drawback. Many government institutions do comply with ERISA, but it is important to check. One benefit of the 403(b) is that the funds that allow employer contributions have shorter vesting periods. *Vesting* refers to the period before an employee is entitled to claim ownership of all employer contributions. Many private-sector companies that offer 401(k)s require employees to work for a certain number of years before they gain ownership of all the employer contributions. Finally, times are changing, but with most 403(b)s, you will generally not have the range of investment options that 401(k)s tend to have. Stocks and real estate investment trusts are prohibited with 403(b)s.

The details of the 401(k) and the 403(b) may be quite

complicated, but companies that offer these retirement plans will have human resource departments or finance departments that assist employees in setting up these accounts and providing further information. If your company offers these retirement plans, it will be easy for you to get started.

The best investment advice that can be offered to any new investor would be to maximize your company 401(k) or 403(b) contributions before investing in any other vehicle. If your contribution is small, plan to try to increase your work retirement contributions over time. All other non-retirement investments will not be subject to tax benefits and, as such, will cost you more.

Finding a Broker

Investment brokers facilitate the transactions between buyers and sellers on the stock exchange. Individual brokers will work for a brokerage firm, but the term *broker* could also apply to the firm itself. Brokers can offer a range of services depending on your investment requirements. Brokers should not be confused with financial planners. A broker will typically be registered with the Financial Industry Regulatory Authority (FINRA) and will specialize in stocks, bonds, and all other securities that are traded on the exchange. They will be qualified to dispense advice on investment strategy and tax as it applies to your investment account. Financial advisors would provide estate planning services, insurance, and general financial-planning assistance. There are also broker-resellers that serve as intermediaries between a broker firm and a client.

Brokers and broker firms will provide the option of either full service, discount service, or both. Full broker service would normally involve higher fees because they will be providing investment advice on an ongoing basis. This advice would be assisted by large research departments that contribute sophisticated market analysis. Using a full-service broker would involve fees for the broker's advice and a charge for every transaction or stock trade that is made. Some brokers may also charge an annual maintenance fee. Full-service brokers tend to also have their own in-house mutual funds which you can invest in without the need for a broker. In this case, your fees would generally be a percentage of the annual returns and not the advisory and transaction fees. Full-service brokers are obviously more costly, and it is up to the individual investor to decide whether they need such services. If you are starting off with small monthly contributions, then a full service may not suit you. Often, people with large investment portfolios that include numerous individual stocks, bonds, and ETFs will see the benefit from using a full service. Full-service fees for advice and transactions can cost between 100 and 200 dollars. The full service is certainly helpful, but if you are concerned about fees, then there are many lower-cost options that are equally good.

Discount service or discount brokers do not offer any advisory or investment planning services. More often than not, they facilitate transactions only, and this is all done online, which reduces costs a great deal. Most discount brokers will offer online resources though, such as market information, which an investor will have access to. Discount brokers will charge between 5 and 30 dollars per trade or transaction. Direct investors who want to manage their own accounts and make their own trades will prefer the discount option. Remember the difference between an investor and a trader. It is not advisable to be trading stocks regularly, in which case your transaction costs should be less frequent with a full- or discount-service broker.

Most broker firms will have a minimum account balance, with discount brokers having the lowest minimum, starting at 500 dollars. Withdrawal fees can also be charged by some brokers. However, if your investment is within a retirement vehicle, you would not want to withdraw your money, and so this may not be a great concern. Whether you select a full service or discount, there will still be companies that charge higher fees than others, which makes it important to compare a number of brokerages before you make your choice.

A new investment option that has come about is the robo-advisor. This is a fully automated investment account that can be used on a computer or as a mobile app. There is almost no human involvement in the process, and all investment decisions are made in line with a client-needs survey. To begin with, you will be asked to complete a survey that will determine your investment needs, such as retirement or short-term saving. Traditional and Roth-style accounts are available as well as non-tax-protected investment accounts. In general, you would not select individual stocks, but rather, a portfolio of ETFs would be selected on your behalf to match your investment goals. Robo-advisor platforms offer a broader range of investment options for more experienced investors with greater balances, but in general, they will pre-select ETFs and sometimes mutual funds because they have the lowest costs. ETFs are also selected because they have been shown to outperform many managed funds over time.

Robo-advisor apps and platforms can be great for investors that are starting off with small amounts because the minimum balances are low, and in some cases, there are no minimum balances. In addition, there are no transaction fees, only a percentage commission of the total account balance, which can be between 0.2 and 0.5%. The saving on fees and commission is a major benefit of robo-advisors, and you should not be scared away because of the fully automated investment process. There will also be what is called *expense ratios*, which are not the robo-advisor fees, but the fees from some of the funds which you may select. Computer software that determines the structure of your investment and re-balances it, depending on market information, is not new. The same technology has been used by formal brokerage firms for some time. Until recently, only brokerage firms could purchase and license the software. Human brokers have been using the same software to assist with their portfolio management since the early 2000s. So, there is no need to be concerned or worried about trusting a robo-advisor to pick your investments.

Many of the online brokerages will also have apps available to investors but will generally be geared towards direct investors that want to manage their own accounts. Most of the online broker apps will also provide an investor with a range of helpful information, such as portfolio analysis, basic investment strategy, and general market tutorials. Many online broker apps will have a minimum account balance of five hundred dollars, but if you shop around, you will find those that have a zero minimum-balance requirement.

Setting Things up

If you have access to a 401(k) or 403(b), and you choose to contribute to it, your payment will be automatically taken from your paycheck and deposited into your account. However, if you are setting up your own investment or retirement account, you have a few options.

When activating an account with a broker, you will need to provide them with your social security number, driver's license, contact information, employment information, and your tax number. Brokerages are, by law, required to ask for all of this information to prevent identity fraud and money laundering. Whether it is online or with a formal brokerage, they will also ask you some questions about your financial goals, your tolerance for risk, and your annual income range. It is not necessary to be precise when stating your income.

You can fund your investment account using an electronic funds transfer (EFT) from your checking or savings account. In addition, you could make a wire transfer or send a check. Transferring money from another broker or from a 401(k) account is also acceptable. Most brokerages will allow you to set up a regular monthly transfer from your checking or savings account so that your contribution is put directly into your investment account just after payday. This is the recommended option because it ensures that you always pay yourself first, which is the primary habit of a successful investor.

The key takeaway from the broker-selection process is the total cost to you and your investment. Brokerages need to make their money somehow, but your goal is to shop around for the best combination of value and low fees. Whether you like the idea of a traditional brokerage, active or passively managed, or an online option, total fees will vary. Sometimes brokers will reveal additional fees in the small print when you begin the account activation process. It is important to know that you are not bound to a broker. You always have the option to withdraw and look for a different broker if the application documents reveal fees which you are not comfortable with.

An example to consider would be the difference of one percent interest on a monthly investment of five hundred dollars over 30 years. One percent less interest paid in fees would result in a loss of over 266,000 dollars at retirement. It demonstrates, again, the power of compound interest and the difference that fees can have on your final investment amount at retirement.

The task of setting up an investment account is a pretty simple process. It is only the type of broker that suits your current needs which requires some thought. Nothing is set in stone though; when your needs change, you can change your type of broker. It's really up to you. We are now ready to move on to strategies. Things are going to get fun and interesting.

Chapter 5: **Goals, Strategies, and Account Types**

Your choice of strategy or combination of investment strategies must align with your goals. You may want to invest purely for retirement, but others will want to invest for retirement and to make a down payment on a house or to fund their kids' college tuition. Long-term investment goals will normally demand a different strategy compared to shorter-term goals.

As we covered in Chapter 3, the general buy-and-hold strategy of long-term investing results in returns that are more closely aligned with the historical market returns. The historical market returns of approximately 10% are considerably higher than the average inflation rate of about 3%. You won't need to be too concerned about short-term ups and downs. When you invest for short periods, though, the ups and downs become more meaningful to you. The market can be fairly volatile when looking at short periods of its history.

To manage risk effectively, the general rule of thumb is to have more conservative investments for your short-term goals and more aggressive investments for your long-term aspirations. Young people who are taking advantage of time have the benefit of utilizing more aggressive investments for their retirement. Older people who are much closer to retirement should be more conservative. This would also apply to people who have been investing for long periods; as you approach retirement, you should look to transfer your investments from aggressive to more safe investments that will protect your money from short-term volatility.

Investing for a mortgage deposit or to subsidize your children's college fees will be shorter investments which would require investment selection that may offer slightly lower average returns, but the returns are more stable over short periods. The differences between aggressive and conservative investments will be covered in detail in Chapter 6. For the moment, more aggressive strategies can be taken to mean that a high percentage of your money is invested in stocks. More conservative investment strategies would mean a good percentage of your money is invested in government bonds and money-market instruments with a lower percentage in stocks.

If you have twin investing goals, retirement, and short term, you will need to have separate investment accounts, which is easily done. Your retirement account will carry tax benefits but also penalties for early access. Your non-tax-protected account will be taxable, but you have the freedom to access your funds whenever you would like.

Types of Accounts

Brokerages will offer three types of accounts to investors in general. You will have a standard taxable account or two retirement accounts that have different tax benefits. If you already have a 401(k) or 403(b), it is advisable to maximize your contribution before opening up an alternative retirement account.

Outside of work retirement plans, the internal revenue service allows for individual retirement accounts (IRAs). These are for people that either don't have 401(k)s available to them or want to invest over and above their work retirement contributions. Like with 401(k)s, IRAs also provide the traditional and Roth options, but contribution rules are different.

Traditional IRAs are tax-deductible in the year in which the contributions were made. However, as of 2021, the maximum tax-free contribution is capped at 6,000 dollars per year, or 500 dollars per month. Workers over the age of 50 years can pay an extra 1,000 dollars per year as a "catch-up" payment. You can access your money from age 59.5 without incurring penalties. Early access carries the same 10% penalty as the 401(k). The exception to the rule would be for medical and educational expenses up to 7.5% of your annual earnings. The traditional IRA also has minimum distribution amounts that come into effect at the age of 72. Between the age of 59.5 and 72, you can withdraw as little or as much as you would like. The basic requirement for an IRA tax deduction is that you earned a taxable income for the year in question. There is one special case where this rule does not apply. If you have a spousal IRA, where you and a spouse file joint tax returns, then only one partner needs to have earned taxable income. In this situation, both partners could contribute their individual maximums.

Roth IRAs have the same contribution maximums as the traditional IRA, but your payments are not deductible. Accessing money from a Roth account is tax-free though, and an added benefit is that there are no penalties for accessing your contributions before retirement age. However, accessing the gains or interest before age 59.5 could trigger income-tax requirements. In addition, there is the five-year rule, which states that you must have had a Roth IRA for five years or longer at retirement in order to benefit from tax-free withdrawals. Another possible benefit is that Roth IRAs do not have minimum distribution rules at any age. This means that you could leave your Roth IRA to grow until your death. Your spouse could inherit your Roth money and would not need to withdraw it either. This is a great benefit for inheritance. A drawback is that there are earnings limits, which prevent some people from accessing Roth IRAs. As of 2021, people who earn less than 198,000 dollars per year can contribute the maximum. Those who earn up to 207,999 dollars can only make partial contributions, and people who earn more than that cannot contribute at all.

An important question is whether you could utilize your maximum 401(k) contribution and IRA contribution in the same year or on an ongoing basis. This can be done but under certain conditions. It can get a bit complicated, but it is worthwhile understanding if you want to maximize your tax-protected investment. If you have selected a Roth 401(k) at work, and you are contributing the maximum, then there is no problem with making the maximum contribution to a Roth IRA in the same year. The only exclusion would be if you earn above 207,999 dollars per year. Earning above that would also disallow you from using a traditional IRA. Any additional investment account that you have in this case would be taxable.

If you are single and you are covered by a 401(k), you can still contribute the maximum to a traditional IRA, provided that you earn less than 66,000 dollars per year. Up to 76,000 dollars, you may make a partial contribution. Earning above that disqualifies you from additional IRA payments. If you are married, and you file joint tax returns, and one of you is covered by a 401(k), then you can still contribute your maximum to a traditional IRA if your combined income as of 2021 does not exceed 197,000 dollars per year. Partial contribution can be made up to the cut-off amount of 207,000 dollars per year.

If you are setting up an additional taxable investment account, then your annual earnings would be subject to capital gains tax. The amount of capital gains tax that you would pay would also depend on your current regular salary tax bracket. However, it is important to be aware of the difference between short-term and long-term capital gains tax. Short-term capital gains arise from the sale of any financial asset that was owned for one year or less. Short-term capital gains provide no tax relief, and your gain is taxed as part of your annual income. Long-term capital gains tax applies to assets that you have held for more than one year. In this case, the capital gains tax brackets are lower, and you are not taxed in line with your current income tax bracket. This is all the more reason to not engage in trading behavior. Holding your stocks in a taxable account for more than a year results in lower taxes. Unless you have a very high annual salary, most people would pay between 0% and 15% long-term capital gains tax.

Cash Versus Margin

Aside from IRA and normal taxable accounts, brokerages also offer a choice between cash and margin accounts. The most commonly used accounts are cash, as margin accounts are generally used by experienced investors. It is important to understand the difference so that you know which account is best for you.

Cash accounts are straightforward. Stocks are only purchased with the cash that you have in your account. If you require additional cash, then some of your existing stock must be sold first in order to purchase new stocks. If your account is with a mutual fund company or all of your money is in managed funds, then you will not need to concern yourself with individual purchases of stocks. If you are a direct investor, and you give your brokerage permission, they can also use your stocks for what is known as *securities lending*. It may sound risky and complicated, but it is actually quite safe.

Other brokerages or investors like to "borrow" stocks for short periods in the hope that they can make a profit from short-term changes in the stock price. You, as the lender, will have a formal contract, where the borrower will provide money to the value of your stock as a guarantee that you will not lose the value of your asset. They are also bound to ensure that you receive any dividends owed to the stock during the borrowing period. Added to this, they will agree to pay you extra interest for the period of borrowing. At the end of the borrowing period, the investor must return your stock plus interest and any dividends that were paid during that time. Essentially, this means that if you hold stocks for the long term, you can allow them to be "lent" out to make additional interest. Any risk involved is taken on by the borrower; you, as the lender, are guaranteed to be given your stock back plus additional interest. This is a way to ensure that you earn growth on your investment over and above the normal dividend payments and growth in value. As a beginner, you may want to keep things simple at first, but securities lending is a good way to maximize your long-term gains.

Margin accounts are a different animal. Margin accounts allow an investor to borrow against the value of the stock that they hold. This is done to purchase new stocks or to engage in securities borrowing. When a margin-account holder engages in securities borrowing, they are effectively doing the opposite of securities lending. The investor is trying to capitalize on the short-term ups and downs of stocks, particularly if they feel that a stock will reduce in value over the short-term. Naturally, this now means that the investor is taking on the risk of borrowing stock. This strategy can be profitable, but it is used by traders or investors that want to make extra short-term profit. A downside of this is that, if an investor with a margin account is running a negative balance due to borrowing, the brokerage is entitled to lend out their stock for securities lending, and the profits are kept by the brokerage. If an investor does not have a negative account balance, then a brokerage is not entitled to use the investor's stock.

Margin accounts and margin investing are considered fairly high risk and remain the territory of traders and professional investors. Being able to sensibly engage in margin trading requires a lot of homework and skill. It will also rack up additional commissions, as these deals are brokered by intermediaries. If you continue to educate yourself and develop in-depth knowledge of the margin game, then it may be an option for you. If you are just finding your feet and only starting to overcome your fear of investing, a standard cash account is the way to go. In time, you could lend your securities out for extra interest with little or no risk to yourself. For starters, that would be the recommended option.

If you have chosen to be an indirect investor and have perhaps selected a robo-advisor as the best option for you, then margins and securities lending will not affect your account. In some cases, robo-advisors do offer more complex account options for individuals with large sums to invest, but normally, if your funds are going to be in ETFs and index funds, margins and securities lending will not be an option.

Chapter 6: What to Buy

We are now at one of the best points of investing. Choosing your individual investments is fun but also extremely important for your personal goals. Before we dive into all of your options, there are two concepts that you must understand first. These two ideas will provide you with a deeper appreciation of investment-portfolio theory, and you will better understand the different options and why investors would choose them and under which circumstances.

Diversification, at its most simple level, is about spreading your money over a range of different stocks and investments in order to cover yourself for market risk. As we covered in Chapter 3, there are currently eleven different sectors in the market, from finance to healthcare and real estate. Over short periods, some sectors will perform much better than others, but over the long run, such as the last one hundred years of the market, the individual sectors perform relatively close to the market average. By spreading your money out over all or most of the sectors, you will be protecting yourself from short-term differences in performance. For example, over a five-year period, the materials sector may be underperforming, but over the same period, the consumer-staples industry has produced great returns. The good returns from consumer staples will offset the underperformance from the materials sector. In this case, the practice of diversification helps to ensure that your invested money has smoother returns over time.

Diversification can go deeper and broader than that, depending on your tolerance for risk. If you were wanting to invest mainly in two sectors that you think were going to perform very well, you would still need to diversify by spreading your money out on many companies in those two sectors. This would be to protect yourself from the reality that some companies within those sectors will perform, producing the majority of returns, but other companies won't perform. Broader diversification would involve not just spreading your money over different sectors of stocks, but also choosing assets like government bonds and money-market instruments.

The second concept is risk. This idea is not just about the possibility of ups and downs in the market. The notion of risk has a more fundamental meaning and impact on potential returns. You may have wondered to yourself why you have to pay higher interest rates when you borrow money compared to, say, a big corporation. You may have to pay higher interest on store credit as opposed to a personal loan from the bank. This is because the lender must be compensated for risk. The greater the perceived risk, the greater the required interest in compensation. For example, if Microsoft wanted to borrow 100,000 dollars, they would present a much lower risk of default compared to a college kid with student debt and a bar job. It may seem counterintuitive that those who can afford it more easily will pay less, but it's purely because they present a lower risk.

As we covered in Chapter 3, when you invest, you are taking on the role of the lender. With most investments, whether a company issues stocks or bonds, they are raising money. They are effectively borrowing money from the market and agreeing to pay a certain interest rate or dividend. You, as the lender, must be compensated for the risk that you take. This is an underlying principle in the market. The greater the return, the greater the corresponding risk. As the lender or investor, you practice diversification to strike a balance between great returns and risk. Unless you are trying to beat the market over time, diversification will be your strategy to secure more reliable returns over your investment period.

Your Options

We will start by looking at bonds and, specifically, government bonds. The bond market is broken up into sectors, including the national bond market, which is further separated into domestic and foreign. Then you have the external bond market, which is sometimes called the Eurobond market. The national bond market includes federal government bonds, local company bonds, and foreign government bonds. The Euromarket is composed of foreign company bonds.

When the government wishes to raise funds for things such as infrastructure projects, they will issue bonds.

The bonds will be issued for a predetermined period and set interest payments will be made generally twice a year. Unlike stocks, the interest payments with bonds are called *coupons* or the *coupon rate*. At the end of the investment period, the government will return the original amount to the lender. Bonds are generally issued for periods of ten years or longer, with ten years being the most common. For example, if you were to purchase a ten-year government bond for 1,000 dollars, which is the face or par value, with a coupon rate of 5%, then you would be paid 2.5% interest on the 1,000 dollars twice a year for ten years. After ten years, which is called the *maturity date*, the government would give you your 1,000 dollars back.

US treasury bonds will pay fairly low coupon or interest rates because they carry almost no risk. In practice, the current US treasury bond interest rate is called the risk-free rate. This is because the government guarantees the capital and the coupon payments. During depressions and many other crises, the government has never defaulted on its payments, which is why a treasury bond is considered to be the closest thing in practice to a risk-free debt. As a result, you, as the potential investor or money lender, do not need to be compensated for any real risk, with the exception of inflation. This is why the 10-year government bond rate will generally be only slightly above the inflation rate. As far as risk is concerned, your money could not be any safer, but the return will be low.

As with stocks, there is a secondary market for government bonds. An investor may have a ten-year bond, but they wish to sell it after four years. What would affect the selling price? Bond prices follow the current interest rate. They have what is called an inverse relationship with the interest rate, which is set by the federal reserve. When interest rates go up, the prices of bonds go down; likewise, when interest rates go down, bond prices go up. To use the same example as before, if you had a 1,000-dollar, ten-year bond with a coupon rate of 5%, and you wanted to sell it after four years, you may sell it for more or less than what you bought it for. This is also because the interest rates and the number of bonds on the market create a supply-and-demand scenario. If interest rates were up when trying to sell your bond, you may only get 990 dollars, but if interest rates are down, and the bond is paying higher rates than the current federal reserve rate, then you may be able to sell your bond for 1,010 dollars. The new owner would still earn their 5% coupon. When a bond sells for below face or par value, it is said to be trading at a discount. If it is selling at above par value, it is trading at a premium.

Corporate bonds work in the same way as government bonds. Their trading or resale value is affected by prevailing interest rates and supply and demand. However, because they are riskier than government bonds, they will pay higher interest rates. Corporate bonds will be given credit ratings that affect the coupon rate that is offered. There are a few credit-rating agencies that have slightly different rating categories, but the basics are the same. The highest credit rating would be AAA, and anything below BBB would be considered a "junk bond." Naturally, junk bonds pay the highest coupon rates. When it comes to coupon payments, there are a few less-common bonds that make what is called a "bullet" payment. This simply means that they do not pay coupons every six months, but rather, they pay back the par value plus all of the coupon payments at maturity in one big amount.

Exchange-traded funds (ETFs) are traded like stocks on the market, but they tend to track sectors, indexes, or a mix of stocks and bonds. An example of an index would be the Standard and Poor's 500 (S&P 500). This is a representation of the top 500 performing stocks on the market. Because the top 500 companies represent all eleven sectors in the economy, the performance of the S&P 500 will closely match the performance of the market. Another example of an ETF would be a bond-tracking fund that covers a range of quality corporate and government bonds. The ETF would aim to track the general performance of the bond market over time. ETFs are considered to be passive investments, as they are not actively managed by a professional team of investors that select stocks. This can provide benefits, as the costs of owning ETFs are lower than managed funds that also attempt to track sectors or the market as a whole. In addition, purchasing ETFs that track the market or purchasing a range of ETFs that track different sectors would provide you with good diversification.

Index funds are similar to ETFs in the sense that they track indexes and diversified mixes of stocks and other investments. They are also passively managed. They differ from ETFs because index funds can only be bought and sold for the price that is set at the end of a trading day. ETFs can be bought and sold at any time during the market trading day. Many brokers will also have minimum investment amounts for index funds that could start at about 2,000 dollars, which is generally more expensive than the cost of an ETF. Robo-advisors and online brokers that have zero minimums would make it easier to invest in index funds if the minimum was a concern. The eleven sectors are listed below.

- Healthcare (pharmaceuticals, medical equipment)
- Utilities (water, electricity distribution)
- Financials (banks, insurance, brokerages)
- Energy (oil and gas)
- Materials (manufacturing, paper, chemicals, timbre)
- Industrials (airlines, railroads, engineering)
- Real Estate (property developers, property managers)
- Information Technology (software, hardware)

- ❏ Communication Services (wireless networks, landline networks)

- ❏ Consumer Staples (food, beverages, tobacco)

- ❏ Consumer Discretionary (luxury goods, leisure products)

Mutual funds are managed by investment professionals. Unlike direct investing, the investor in a mutual fund would not own any of the stocks or bonds within the fund. The fund would pool all investors' money in order to purchase assets on behalf of the fund. An individual investor would then have what are called *shares* in the fund. The value of your shares would rise as the value of the fund increases. For example, if you were to put your monthly 500-dollar contribution into a mutual fund, then on a monthly basis you would be credited with 500 dollars of shares in the fund. If the total fund earned 10% interest for a year, your total share value would increase by 10%. Mutual fund companies offer a range of different types of funds that cater to different investors' needs. You would have access to funds that are composed entirely of mixed stocks, while some funds will be comprised of real estate stocks only. For safer investing, there would also be funds that consist mainly of government and corporate bonds. As with an index fund, the returns on a mutual fund would be the average of all of its individual investments. The fund managers would take care of the diversity requirements, but an individual investor could further diversify by separating their contributions between different mutual funds. All mutual funds will have historic performance reports available to potential investors, which would allow you to see how a fund has performed over time. This is helpful for comparisons when taking into account the funds fees and general performance.

The money market or money-market funds involve the short-term debt market. Governments, companies, and even banks may want to borrow money for short periods of time. Short-term lending can be anywhere from one day to 270 days. Because the lending periods are short, and there is generally less risk in lending over shorter periods, money-market investments do not pay high returns. Similar to government and high-credit-rated bonds, money-market investments are considered to be safer, with lower but more reliable returns.

Real estate investment trusts (REITs) are similar to mutual funds in their composition, but they are traded like stocks on the exchange. A real estate trust or company would own, finance, or manage a portfolio of real estate assets. As an investor, you may not have enough money to purchase real estate directly but would be able to buy a share in the real estate portfolio by owning REITs. The investor in REITs would earn interest payments, and the value of the REIT itself could also increase over time. One drawback with REITs is that they tend to focus on specific sectors within real estate, such as malls or office buildings, which can be bad for diversification. A possible strategy would be to invest in a number of REITs that, combined, cover most of the real estate sector.

A name that you may have come across is "penny stocks." No doubt, your immediate thoughts may be negative. Penny stocks are defined as any stock that trades for five dollars or less on the market. Some penny stocks are traded on the New York Stock Exchange, but most are traded over-the-counter (OTC) on an electronic bulletin board. Your typical penny stock is a startup business or a fairly small company. The brokers that promote them will almost always suggest the idea of mind-boggling returns. The problems with penny stocks are numerous. The market for penny stocks is not as liquid as normal stocks, meaning that they can be a lot harder to sell. With less general trade, it is also harder to determine the real value of a penny stock because the supply-and-demand process does not function as well. You also need to consider the statistics for startups. About 90% of them fail, with only 40% of them ever turning a profit.

Professional investors generally don't look at startups. Mutual fund managers in particular will always wait for a company to develop a track record that can be analyzed. Typically, this would mean that a company would have to have been around for a good five years before a fund manager would start to examine it more closely. You may wonder why any investor would look to a penny stock company. Firstly, you can buy a lot of their stock cheaply, and they promise great returns. People tend to reference the story of Amazon, which is the most successful penny stock of all time. In 1997, Amazon first sold its shares as a little-known company for around two dollars apiece. Today, in 2021, those shares are selling for around 3,340 dollars each. Apple is another example. In the early 2000s, its stock sold for a whopping 80 cents. As of today, it sells for 134 dollars and has been paying dividends of between 1.60 and 2.60 dollars per stock every year. This is the temptation with penny stocks; people are hoping to invest in the next Amazon or Apple. For every Amazon, there are hundreds of startups that crash or return no profit. Professional investors find it hard to tell the difference between an Amazon and a stinker in a company's first few years. As a personal wealth investor, you would be wise to avoid penny stocks. It is often said that the only people who make money from penny stocks are the brokers who originally sell them.

Diversification Examples

In theory, an investor could diversify their investment portfolio in an infinite number of ways. In this section, you will be presented with a number of practical examples of how a portfolio could be diversified, depending on your investment goals. There will be a typical example for a young person who has decades of retirement investing ahead of them. There will also be examples for people who are starting later in life and for people who have now reached retirement and are looking to preserve the wealth that they have gained. The examples will serve as guidelines that do not have to be adhered to precisely, but they will serve to give you a better understanding of how diversification is combined with different investment goals in practice.

If you have opted to invest in managed funds, such as mutual funds, then these examples will provide you with a guideline for the types of mutual funds that you should select in order to match your investments with your goals and strategy. In the case of a robo-advisor, your investment selection will be ETFs, but in principle, the ETF selections should be comparable with the examples.

Regardless of your investment needs or whether you engage in direct or indirect investment, it will be assumed that you will always be reinvesting your dividends in order to earn compound interest. If you allow yourself to get into the habit of spending your dividend or coupon payments, then you will be dramatically reducing your long- term wealth potential. In addition, almost all mutual funds, ETFs, bonds, and index funds, when posting their historic performance statistics, will always state the average returns assuming that an investor has reinvested their returns. For example, when the estimated returns on a ten-year bond are stated, it is always assumed that the investor will be reinvesting their coupon payment over the ten-year period. Failing to do this will result in a return that is much lower than the stated yield or return. By now, the pay-yourself-first attitude should also make sense, so we will assume that you will have an automatic bank transfer set up to fund your account on a monthly basis, making the habit of investing that much easier.

There are three broad categories of investment strategies that we will cover. They are aggressive, balanced, and defensive investments. Young people who have the luxury of riding out short-term market movements should be selecting more aggressive investment portfolios. Aggressive investments will allow you to maximize your wealth creation over the span of a long working career. Closer to retirement, you could look to transfer your money or rebalance your investment for a balanced or defensive strategy so that your money is not subject to big ups and downs when you are retired. The general thinking is that you have created your wealth while you were working. In retirement, you are preserving it. Below is an example of an aggressive fund.

- 98% stocks (35% foreign stocks)

- 2% money market

In the aggressive investment, almost all of your money is in stocks, with a good portion in foreign stocks as well. If you are looking to use a mutual fund, the aggressive mutual funds will be similar in composition. The stock percentage may be a little bit lower, but this is what a mutual fund company would call an equity fund and would suggest it if you expressed the need for an aggressive fund. The relative diversity would be in place by the fund distributing the pool of money in more or less equal portions amongst the eleven sectors.

Periodically, the balance between the sectors could change in order to accommodate sectors that are performing better than others.

If you are investing directly, your purchases would match the above percentages, but you could add a number of ETFs that index the market and some of the individual sectors for diversity. This is a good option because a mutual fund has a great deal more money with which to buy stocks. As an individual, you could own a number of stocks, but having ETFs will be a cost-effective way of diversifying and reducing your transaction fees. Perhaps half of your money could be in individual stocks that you have confidence in, while the other half of your money is in ETFs or index funds. ETFs would be a good way to cover your foreign-stocks component in an affordable way. A good example of an ETF that tracks a foreign market is the Franklin FTSE Europe ETF. The Franklin ETF is diversified in such a way that it tracks the performance of the top medium- to large-sized companies in the European market.

Selecting an aggressive investment option with a robo-advisor would result in a similar makeup. However, your portfolio would be ETFs that track the market and sectors. Over time, the portfolio would also be rebalanced with fewer or more ETFs covering the different sectors.

A balanced portfolio would be more suitable for an investor that is starting much later, perhaps in their late forties. This is because a more balanced portfolio would be subject to much smaller ups and downs over the duration of the investment. If you have less than twenty years to retirement, avoiding the possibility of larger swings in the market would be best. Likewise, if you are engaging in short- to medium-term investing for a mortgage deposit or for your child's college tuition, a balanced portfolio would also be a good strategy. Below is a guideline for a balanced portfolio.

- 68% stocks (15% foreign)

- Bonds 15%

- Real estate 10%

- Money market 7%

If you were investing in mutual funds, the above example would be typical of a balanced, or short- to medium-term, investment portfolio. The stock component may still be fairly high, but there is now a bond and money-market percentage that provides safety, but lower returns. The bond component would be diversified between domestic government bonds, good foreign government bonds, and company bonds with the highest credit ratings. The real estate component would be diversified through direct investment in property, such as malls, but also in REITs and real estate index funds. Naturally, the stocks would also be separated out amongst the eleven sectors.

As a direct investor, your portfolio would roughly mirror the above example. Again, because a mutual fund has a large amount of money to invest, to achieve the same level of diversification, you could use index funds and ETFs to match the basic percentages. For example, you could have 15% of your money invested in ETFs that track the performance of the bond market. Your real estate component could be made up of a few stocks but mainly REITs that track sectors within real estate. You could also make up your money-market portion through ETFs or index funds. To strike a balance between transaction cost and diversification, you could purchase a range of stocks directly that you like but make up the foreign, bond, and money-market portion with ETFs and index funds.

A defensive investment portfolio would suit an investor that has already created their wealth and is now in retirement. A retiree that is satisfied with their savings would want to ensure that their retirement income is extremely safe and not subject to the nature of the market. These portfolios are for investors that are happy to sacrifice returns for reliability. Below is an example of a defensive portfolio.

- Stocks 40%
- Bonds 35%
- Real estate 12%
- Money market 13%

The defensive portfolio has a much higher percentage of bonds and money-market instruments. Stocks, however, are not completely removed. A reasonable stock component is still required for balance and diversity. If all of your money were to be in bonds and the money market, then your average returns would be only marginally better than inflation. With a defensive portfolio, approximately fifty percent of your money is in safe, reliable assets. Depending on whether you had a Roth or traditional account, you may have to pay tax on your retirement income. If you were to have a portfolio that was making only a little above inflation, when combined with taxes and fees, you could be losing. When you enter this phase of your investing journey, and you are simply protecting your wealth, then fees on these types of portfolios become particularly important.

The use of low fee ETFs to help create this portfolio composition would become more advisable. If you are using a mutual fund for a defensive portfolio, then the fees versus the historical returns of the fund will be especially important.

The above examples demonstrate diversification in practice. The concept of diversification is simple but is relative to the kind of investment strategy that you choose. There certainly can be examples of over-diversification. Thinking that you can never have too much diversification can also lead to lower returns. For example, if you are a self-directed investor, and you maximize your IRA contribution of 500 dollars per month, your stock purchases will be limited on a monthly basis. Choosing to purchase a different stock every month for decades would result in your owning a few thousand individual stocks. This would be overkill, and it would beg the question: How well have you looked at each company stock before buying if you have thousands of stocks? There is no strict limit to the number of stocks that you should invest in, but a helpful guideline would be to limit yourself to no more than a few hundred at the most. Broad diversification can be achieved by having some ETFs that cover the market and a few major sectors.

Chapter 7: **Things to Avoid**

With your newfound knowledge of the market and your potential to create wealth, you are now empowered to enter the world of investing with confidence and a more realistic understanding of market risk. There are, however, mistakes that even experienced investors can still make. Developing the habit of paying yourself first is one part of your "head game." Your attitude and mindset over time is the other part. Being excited about your investment journey is a good thing, but it is important to remain grounded. Many newcomers to investing can start with unrealistic expectations. If you are investing for the long haul, and you have a well-structured portfolio, there will be some limits as to how big your returns will be. The example of Warren Buffet is a great one for driving home the point. As one of the greatest investors of all time, his career track record is an average return of 20% per year. This was achieved through a very skillful strategy but also one that was not reckless. Warren Buffet believed in investing for the long haul and never chased quick scores. An average return of 20% would mean doubling his money approximately every three and a half years. That's what arguably the greatest investor in history could achieve, reliably and safely. If your average return over a good period of time matches the market average, you have done well for yourself. Attempting to match or beat Warren Buffet is unrealistic. The goal of matching the market return after fees and commissions is a better target to set your sights on.

Avoid making the mistake of not diversifying properly. If you are purchasing individual stocks, then having stocks in only one or two companies per sector is inadequate. If you lack the funds to diversify properly in stocks, then cover yourself with indexed ETFs. Some companies may seem to be growing from strength to strength, but that is no reason to put most of your money in just a few companies, no matter how stable you may think they are.

Common Errors

If you have decided to be a passive investor in a mutual fund company or have opted for a full brokerage service, then a number of common errors can be avoided. The downside is that a full brokerage service will be more expensive in terms of fees. Direct investors will need to be particularly aware of some of the common mistakes that are made by beginners and experts alike.

An investor should prevent emotions from governing their decisions. Your emotions can be triggered by events such as dips in the market or in sectors. If you are a long-haul investor, you should see the dips in the market as an opportunity to purchase stocks at a cheaper price that will give you greater returns over time. When you respond to every short-term dip, without realizing it, your investment behavior starts to resemble that of a trader. Selling with high frequency changes the basic and simple strategy of buying and holding.

Another emotional form of investing is developing too much of an attachment to one or a few companies. If you are going to pick individual stocks, your choices must be based on more than a company's image or the fact that you like its products and services. If you do not have the ability to develop a deeper understanding of companies and how they will make their future profits, then it is best to be impartial and diversify.

You should also evaluate your investment purchases on a regular basis to ensure that you are sticking to your game plan over time. If you are investing fairly small amounts on a monthly basis, then you may not be able to purchase stocks and assets every month that match the percentage of your desired portfolio strategy. For example, if you are pursuing a balanced portfolio for a mortgage deposit, your monthly contribution may not afford you the ability to buy 68% stocks, 15% bonds, and 7% money market. It may take you a few months to purchase the assets in the right ratios. This is something that you will need to monitor to ensure that, over time, your portfolio has the correct diversification.

In Chapter 2, we covered the issue of investing while also paying off debt. Debt can be unavoidable, but it must always be separate from your investing habit. It is never a good idea to borrow money in order to invest. Borrowing to invest in your first home is a notable exception, but to borrow money to buy stocks is very risky. Margin accounts allow you to borrow against your own money, although this practice is better left to more experienced investors.

Make an effort to not follow the crowd. Often there can be media buzz surrounding a particular stock, but in most cases, when the media covers a stock, it has already achieved its growth limit, or the media hype results in a flurry of purchases that artificially raises the value of the stock. You should be especially wary of "experts" or investment "gurus" that promote a penny stock as the next biggest thing. These will most certainly be costly errors for an investor. As a general rule, when there is a great deal of hype surrounding a stock that you have never heard of, it is best to exercise caution or to avoid it altogether.

Over the course of your investing, make sure that you invest more if you can afford to do so. Aside from increasing your investment contribution when you get a better-paying job, idle cash should also be invested. If you have money left at the end of a year that you do not need for expenses or quality of life, top up your investment account. The top up contributions that you make over time will make a difference to your retirement or shorter-term goals.

What Makes a Good Investor?

The traits of good investors may seem more relevant to people who have chosen to manage their own accounts. You may say to yourself that, if you are investing in mutual funds or with a robo-advisor that balances your investments for you, then thinking about the market is not really necessary. Managed funds are a perfectly good investment vehicle, but that does not mean that you can invest and forget. It remains important for you to keep an eye on your wealth, especially as you draw nearer to retirement or your other goals. Having a good idea of where you are in your long-term goal can also help with occasional adjustments. Tracking your wealth on an annual basis could signal a need to increase your contribution, or it could just give you peace of mind that your goals are on track.

Direct investors, and even experts, need to recognize the need for ongoing learning. This book has provided you with a great foundation, but successful direct investors will never stop acquiring new and updated knowledge about the market or the companies that they invest in. Keeping your ear to the ground will hold you in good stead.

Be confident in your abilities as an investor but avoid the temptation of material displays of success. All too often, when investors see that they have made good gains, there is a need to reward themselves by splurging on luxuries. Achieving greater-than-expected returns simply means that you will hit your goals earlier or you will exceed them.

Acquiring your own knowledge is vital, but the best investors will still seek help or a second opinion when they need it. Your investment broker may offer a great range of tools and resources to aid in your learning, but do not rely on them as your only source of knowledge. Seeking out the opinions of others does not mean that you have to accept their advice in every instance. Rather, it broadens your view of the market and exposes you to information or thinking which you might not have considered yourself.

Good investors also know when to accept their mistakes. As much as a buy-and-hold strategy is the way to go, you may see, over time, that a certain company has not performed. Sticking with a poor performer when it has demonstrated low or negative returns over years should be avoided. It may sound obvious, but many investors have difficulty accepting that they misjudged a stock. It is not uncommon for investors in these cases to invest further in that stock, thinking they are getting stock at a reduced price. It may temporarily mask the loss, but in the long run, you are sacrificing other great stock opportunities. The opposite of this common trait is keeping winners. Great stocks can give really good returns and rise in value. This does not mean that you should sell them to earn a great profit. The lure of cashing in on a great performer will bring immediate gains but cost you wealth over your investing journey.

All of this advice may seem pretty obvious, particularly in light of what you have learned so far. However, reality would seem to differ from theory with many people. There is a good body of research on direct investors that demonstrates that high numbers of investors do not apply the basics. On the surface, these investors know and understand the general strategies required for success, but somehow, they stray. Their investment accounts are characterized by frequent selling and poor diversity. They pay transaction fees regularly, and they hold bad stocks. What conclusions can be drawn from this? Perhaps, over time, they convince themselves that they know enough to discard the rules. Maybe the desire to beat the market clouds their judgment. They could be neglecting the advice and outside opinions of others.

Either way, it is a common enough problem to warrant you thinking about the basics often. Always give yourself a reality check. Investing is simple, and complicating matters creates delusions. When purchasing a stock, you should ask yourself what your thinking is. Would you feel comfortable explaining your choice to another person?

Chapter 8: **This Is Just the Beginning**

In the investment world, there are other alternatives that can be a bit more complex. If you are comfortable with applying the basics and sticking to the beaten path, you will achieve your wealth goals. If, at some point, you feel that you are ready to take on a more complex range of investments, then this chapter will open your eyes to the possibilities. Some of the alternatives will carry a lot of potential risk. If you are interested in exploring these options, then a good word of advice would be to use non-retirement-investment income. There are many investors who like to take bigger risks, but they compartmentalize their investing. They make sure that they are contributing sufficient funds to their retirement and other goals using the buy-and-hold philosophy. Money that they have left over after paying themselves first is what they use to make riskier investments that require a trading strategy.

A class of alternative investment would be the derivatives market. The three main categories of derivatives are known as futures, options, and swaps. Put simply, these investments are used to cover an investor for the risk of price movements in stocks or assets, either up or down. The world of derivatives can seem overly complicated because it has its own set of jargon. The ins and outs of futures, options, and swaps will be discussed using jargon only when necessary. Investors will use derivatives mainly to "hedge" their bets or speculate on price and market movements. Just like with margin accounts, investors may want to have a "long" or a "short" stake in a stock, or both. The long stake means that you own the stock and hold it for long periods. The short position is to own or borrow the stock to capitalize on short-term ups and downs in the stock price. In order to cover you from either outcome, whether the stock rises or dips, the investor would use a derivative to protect themselves from an unexpected outcome. For example, you could have a farmer who enters into a futures contract with a buyer in February. The farmer wishes to sell his cotton at 5.5 dollars per bushel in July. The current value of a bushel of cotton is 5.5 dollars but the farmer believes that the price will lower come July, and he is concerned about his total revenue for the season. If the farmer is right and in July the price of cotton has fallen to 5 dollars per bushel, the buyer will have to purchase them for 5.5 dollars. If, however, he is wrong and cotton rises in July to 6 dollars, then the buyer wins and is entitled to purchase the cotton for 5.5 dollars per bushel. This is one of the simpler examples of a derivative type of contract, but it demonstrates the basic principle that underlies the use of all of the different derivative instruments.

Derivative contracts are created and traded in two types of markets. There is the exchange-traded (ET) derivative and the over-the-counter (OTC) variety. The exchange-traded variety of derivatives is standardized and has fixed contract terms to facilitate easy trade on the market. The OTC derivatives are individually negotiated to meet the specific requirements of an investor. The OTC derivatives can be sold by the original buyer, but they are far less liquid due to the tailor-made nature of them. ET derivatives are very liquid and can be purchased and resold with ease. In addition, ET derivatives are guaranteed by the exchange's clearing house, which makes the risk of default by either party less likely than with the OTC variety. Small-scale investors would generally stick to the ET variety because it makes smaller transactions far simpler.

A futures contract is an agreement to either buy or sell a stock or asset at a predetermined price on a set date in the future. There is what is called the *spread*, which is the difference between the expected price on the date in the future and the possible range of difference both up and down that could occur. The methods that are used to calculate the spread and the value of the future are quite complex, but the spreads are generally not too large; otherwise, it would be difficult to get two parties to agree on a set price. For example, if a seller of oil wanted to lock in a selling price of 100 dollars per barrel in six months from now, the potential buyer would also have to be confident that they were making a good deal. You could not thumb-suck a selling price; it would have to be based on some underlying method of reasoning that both parties can understand. This is one type of trading activity that you could engage in if you had a margin account with your broker, as opposed to a standard account. An example of what is called a *long* position with futures would involve an investor at the beginning of a year deciding that they will purchase 100 shares of Tesla at 100 dollars each on May 15th. If the market value of Tesla stock goes up before May 15th, the investor could sell their future contract for a profit. The futures contract had a price of 10,000 dollars (100 x 100). If Tesla stocks rose in value to 110 dollars each, the futures contract could be sold for 11,000 dollars, earning a profit of 1,000 dollars. The short position would apply to an investor that had a future contract to sell their stocks. The short position is used when an investor thinks that a stock price will fall in the short run.

An options contract is similar to a future except that the owner of an option is not obligated to exercise it. An investor could have an agreement to purchase or sell a stock on a set date in the future for a specific price, but they could choose to not sell or buy. Naturally, this option comes at a price to the owner. With both options and futures, particularly with stocks, there will be a purchase price and transaction fees that need to be taken into account. Options and futures are available for stocks, bonds, and indexes such as the S&P 500. All commodities are also covered, such as oil, gold, silver, diamonds, wood, and rubber. When a buyer has the right or option to purchase an asset at a set price, it is referred to as a *call option*. In the opposite case, when a seller has the right to sell at a set price, it is called a *put option*.

A *swap* is a derivative contract between two parties that agree to exchange liabilities or cash flows, such as dividends, from two different financial assets or instruments. These types of derivative contracts are always OTC in nature and never traded on the exchange. The most common form of swap agreement is with interest rates, but they can be used with commodities, currency, and what are called *total return swaps*. An example of a total return swap could involve a pool of stocks. The owner of the stocks may enter into a swap agreement to be guaranteed a set return or interest payment over a period of time. The other party to the agreement would get the dividend payments from the stocks and the increase in stock value. In this case, the owner of the stocks is forfeiting potential earnings in order to get a guaranteed return. The other party to the agreement takes a risk that the dividends and stock value might be less than the set amount that they are paying. Then again, the dividends and stock value increase may be more over the period, in which case they make a profit.

A commodity swap is similar in principle. One party may agree to pay the changing price for oil over a period of a year, while the other party is given a set price for oil for the year. The party with the set price now has certainty as to what they will pay. The other party is now taking the risk of the price fluctuation in oil over the year, but they could also profit if average prices are below the set price.

Cryptocurrency, Forex, and Commodities Trading

Cryptocurrency is virtual money that exists entirely online. One of its selling points is that it cuts out the need for a bank or middleman that will charge a transaction fee or commission. This makes payments and, in particular, international payments, quick and costless. If you think of a payment solution like PayPal, cryptocurrency serves a similar purpose: to facilitate financial transactions, except cryptocurrency is the method of payment itself.

The notable difference between paying in traditional ways is that cryptocurrency transactions are not reversible, and they are anonymous. They also do not have the same protection as money does that is stored in banks and credit unions. If you are storing cryptocurrency in an online wallet, and the company goes bankrupt, or your account is hacked, you will simply lose your cryptocurrency.

Unlike a federal government that controls the supply of money, a cryptocurrency is produced by its system at a rate that is defined when the system is created. The individual currency is called a "coin," and all or a portion of it would be used to purchase other items or assets. Just like the market, the value of a coin or a specific cryptocurrency is largely based upon scarcity and supply and demand. Due to the high number of available cryptocurrencies, the overall viability of the individual company and cryptocurrency system can also affect its perceived value. As of early 2021, Bitcoin was the most valuable cryptocurrency, with one Bitcoin being worth 46,000 dollars. Bitcoin is also the most commonly used currency, although cryptocurrencies are fairly new and have not gained universal acceptance. To date, approximately 36% of small- to medium-size companies in the US accept Bitcoin as a form of payment. In all other cases, intermediaries are needed, such as with the new Bitcoin debit cards. Other popular cryptocurrencies, like Ethereum, are mainly accepted by online companies.

Bitcoin's growth in value has been characterized by a series of bubbles, with the daily value fluctuating up and down by fairly large amounts. However, if you consider that Bitcoin has only been in existence since 2010, and its starting value was 0.0008 dollars, its ultimate rise in value has been impressive. This may be due to new factors that have caused some investors to look to Bitcoin. Originally, Bitcoin was introduced purely as a digital currency that was outside the control of any one country. Over time, Bitcoin has seen increases in demand and value in times when the traditional market is down. Some investors are starting to treat Bitcoin as though it were gold. Historically, investors have turned to gold when they feel that their currency is unstable. As it stands, cryptocurrency has not gained mainstream acceptance with investors, but perhaps its use as a store of value during economic slumps may contribute to its longevity.

You can invest directly in a cryptocurrency by purchasing a coin or a portion of a coin using a trading app. New indirect methods have come about such as

ETFs and index funds. There are specific Bitcoin ETFs that track the performance of Bitcoin-related companies and cryptocurrency indexes, such as Bitwise 10, that tracks the ten largest cryptocurrency values. Because cryptocurrencies are new, and their values have been subject to large rises and dips, investing in cryptocurrency is risky, and like with all risky investments, any potential investor should conduct thorough research before getting into the game.

Forex is short for the foreign exchange market, where foreign currencies are traded with one another. The value of individual currencies is also determined by supply and demand, with a small number of exceptions where a government may artificially set the value of its currency. The overwhelming majority of currencies are "free-floating," meaning that natural supply and demand determine their value at any given time. When a company wishes to import a product or material from Britain, they will need to pay for it in British pounds. Likewise, when a British company purchases American products or services, they are paid for in US dollars. The total of these transactions is the demand for the currency. If the demand from Americans for British pounds is greater than the demand from Britons for Dollars, then the value of a pound will be greater relative to the dollar. Like with stocks, the values of currencies are subject to rises and dips, with small daily changes being common. Dramatic reductions in the demand for a currency will result in a corresponding decline in value. There are many reasons why a currency could experience a steady reduction in value over time. It could be brought about by political instability, declining investor confidence, or heavy government debt.

When people refer to the Forex market, they generally mean what is called the "spot market," which is an OTC online market where foreign currency is bought and sold at its current price at that moment. The spot market is the largest avenue for investors and traders in currency. There is also a healthy derivatives market which is mainly used by companies that want to protect themselves from the risk of currency fluctuation. For example, an American company may sell a product in Britain for one hundred pounds, which is a competitive price. The current exchange rate may be 1.6 dollars to the pound. If the pound loses value, then when the profit is converted back to dollars, the American company will suffer a reduction in final dollar profit. This is where a company would use a derivative contract to secure pre-determined exchange rates between the dollar and the pound.

Traders in Forex will attempt to make profits on the spot market by trying to capitalize on price changes between currencies. They could have short-term strategies whereby they seek to make a profit on the daily dips and rises in currency value, or they could play a longer game if they feel that a currency will gain value against another currency over time. For example, a trader may purchase 10,000 euros at an exchange rate of 1.17, which costs 11,700 dollars. If the exchange rate changes over the following two weeks to 1.26, then the euros can be sold for 12,600 dollars, resulting in a profit of 900 dollars.

The actual trading of currency on the Forex market is very similar to that of stocks. There will also be bids and asks, and traders take either long or short positions. The long position is buying a currency, and the short position is the selling of a currency. Forex trading for profit is considered to be speculative, meaning it is risky. Understanding how to read the rises and dips of various currencies is a skill. Most Forex trading accounts will also offer practice accounts which allow newcomers to place trades in a real-world scenario without actually using their money. Spending a good amount of time on a practice account is advisable to ensure that you are confident in your knowledge and understanding.

Commodities trading differs from investing in the commodities sector through stocks. Traders and individual investors will typically use the commodities derivative market to trade. This is because traditional commodities trading involves the sale and physical delivery of the commodity, such as coal or wheat. Traders wishing to gain from price changes without actually having to take delivery of the commodity in question will trade in futures contracts. The trader will aim to make a profit on the change in the value of the futures contract and will typically sell the futures contract before its expiry date to avoid having to take physical possession of the commodity. Not all brokers engage in commodities trading, which may require an investor to open a separate trading account. There are varying minimum balances for the accounts, and all commodities-trading accounts will be margin accounts.

This section has provided a brief introduction to derivatives and cryptocurrency. It may have piqued your interest, but it must be re-emphasized: Your retirement goals should always come first. Commodities trading is mostly conducted by full-time traders who do it for a living. They live and breathe the commodities market and have a deep understanding of the risks involved. Other investors dabble in commodities trading more as a hobby. The old adage of "don't bet the farm" applies to derivatives trading in general. If you have some spare cash that you can afford to lose, then exploring commodities and derivatives can be challenging and fun. Keep your retirement and other investment goals separate.

Direct Real Estate Investing

Direct real estate investment requires more starting cash than investing in REITs or real estate stocks. A large number of people will be direct investors in real estate by simply buying a house and paying off the mortgage. Investing directly in real estate is the one investment where you would generally not be able to avoid borrowing money in order to get into the game. However, there are ways for beginner investors to make a success of it and earn a steady income and asset growth. These days, it is not even necessary to invest in a second property to earn income from real estate.

Direct investing can be done through traditional buying to rent, online investing platforms, and property flipping. Alternative options involve individual room rentals and occasional rentals using a service such as Airbnb. The fundamental consideration when purchasing a property to rent is to have an accurate idea of what the maintenance costs and mortgage fees will be. The rule of thumb is that the monthly rental should be able to cover your total costs.

In practice, finding a property where the monthly rental that you can charge is one percent of the purchase price is difficult, but it is a guideline for your investment choice. The closer that you can get to the one percent mark, the better. Real estate also requires work and knowledge, and a majority of successful investors will specialize within a sector of real estate. For example, you could look to the affordable-housing market or to flats. Specialization often involves sticking to specific areas or neighborhoods where you have acquired sound knowledge.

The factors to consider when purchasing a house to rent, or for your own use, are the same. The neighborhood that you choose will determine the type of tenants that you can attract. The quality of the surroundings is an important factor not just in terms of tenants, but for the potential growth in value over time. Things such as schools, public facilities, good transport, low crime, and a low turnover rate are all good features to look out for. The turnover rate refers to the number of houses that are vacant or on sale in the area. If an area has vacant houses or people that have moved out frequently, it could be a sign of underlying problems that could negatively impact your property value in the long run. If a neighborhood is on a slow decline, it could also affect the quality of the tenants that you could attract.

It's also important to find out how much property tax will need to be paid. Often, people do not include property taxes in their calculations of costs, which can turn a possible good buy into a bad one. An idea for young investors would be to buy a property that is suitable for student accommodation or young workers. A three- or four-bedroom house with a design that could suit communal living would be ideal. An investor could live in one room and rent out the other three. If the monthly rental from your three tenants covers all of your costs, namely utilities, mortgage, maintenance, and taxes, then you are set. You will be a homeowner, and your tenants will be paying your mortgage for you.

Property flipping is the practice of buying a house for the short-term and selling it on for a profit. Generally speaking, an investor will look for properties that are slightly undervalued and perhaps need some renovation work in a decent area. They will also have an idea of the price trends for the area and will be certain that general property values are going upward. Unlike a buy-and-hold strategy, a property flipper would want to sell the investment as quickly as possible to avoid ongoing mortgage and property tax costs.

A standard guideline that is used by property flippers is the 70% rule. The investor would need to be able to accurately cost the renovations required in order to calculate what a house's after-repair value (ARV) is. The investor would not buy a house for more than 70% of the ARV, minus the cost of repairs. For example, if a house that is fixed up nicely could sell for 200,000 dollars, and the renovation needed would be 25,000 dollars, then you should not be willing to pay more than 115,000 dollars to buy. Property flipping is a skill, and the common errors that new investors make are underestimating the costs of renovation and how long the house may be on the market. Taking time to make yourself knowledgeable and understanding a sector and a few neighborhoods is essential. In 2019, approximately 6% of houses sold were "flipped" houses. Clearly, there are more than enough investors engaging in the practice. Many are successful.

Online platforms for crowdfunding are a new way for investors to buy directly into a property. Before the JOBS act, real estate investors were only allowed to invest in REITs or buy property themselves. Previously, only institutional investors, such as banks, could buy and own portions of real estate investments such as malls and office complexes. Crowdfunding has now made it possible for real estate companies to raise funding from many investors, providing small amounts each. All investors, regardless of the size of their contribution, become shareholders, or part owners, of the properties and are entitled to their share of the rental profits. In the case of the property being sold, all investors would get their share of the proceeds. In the case of a crowdfunded real estate company going public and listing on the stock exchange, the investors would stand to make a good sum of money.

Minimum contributions can vary from 1,000 to 5,000 dollars, which is a far lower amount compared to what accredited investors had to contribute before the JOBS act, where minimum amounts could be as much as ten million dollars. A small investor is now able to own a direct stake in large investment properties that can generate returns that rival the stock market. The main risk involved is that real estate companies that raise money through crowdfunding tend to be new and do not have a track record that an investor could analyze.

The Securities and Exchange Commission (SEC) has introduced limits for the amounts that non-institutional investors can contribute to crowdfunded real estate investments. If your annual income or net worth is less than 107,000 dollars, then you would be permitted to invest the greater of 2,200 dollars or five percent of your annual income. If an investor has a net worth or income of more than 107,000, then their annual contribution would be capped at ten percent of their annual earnings.

Some areas of investing are changing as new innovations and technologies emerge. Some new investment vehicles are being embraced by the mainstream finance community. Others are taking their time to gain universal acceptance. Staying with the tried and trusted methods of investment will serve you well. If you have developed a newfound interest in all of the possibilities, then move forward with caution. Your job will be to dive deeper and to never stop learning.

Conclusion

So, is the market scary? You have learned that it is no more frightening than taking a bus to work or driving to your local mall. Yes, there can be risks, but they are understandable and manageable. If you adhere to the rules of the road, your investment journey will end with wealth and a comfortable retirement.

The real bogeyman is inflation. Year after year, inflation eats at the value of money and must be beaten. Leaving all of your money in a standard bank savings account is little better than burying your money in the backyard. Investing is not just advisable; it is essential for everyone. People are living longer and longer. Retirement will be either a pleasant time to enjoy your golden years, or it can be a period of hardship and stress. The route to achieving your wealth goals and living a life of financial control is simple in principle. You don't need to be a Wall Street banker to know enough to invest and to be successful at it.

The power of compound interest demonstrates how valuable it is to start young. What seems like trivial amounts of money grows into a lot. The habit of investing, or paying yourself first, is the important first step. Before you have picked a stock or investigated a mutual fund, you need to be on top of your personal finances. Know how much you need to be investing to meet your goals. You do not need to live the life of a pauper to create wealth further down the line. Quality of life is important to all of us, and we need to spend money on things that give us pleasure. However, once you have calculated your goals, they are a priority that you must stick to for the long haul. The habit of investing every month is the vital ingredient.

You have learned that you can afford to invest, even if you are young or your spare money does not seem enough. There are many simple ways to free up investment money, from maximizing your tax deductions to renting out a room in your flat or avoiding store credit. A few less beers every month or one less night out is all it takes to start. As you get older, you may earn more money, but your expenses will also increase. There will never be a better time than now.

The stock market is not an unknowable entity of fear. It is understandable, and the basic principles that drive it are easy to grasp. Supply and demand is a concept that affects many aspects of our lives, not just the market. The US stock exchange has been around for some two hundred years and will remain for centuries to come. The historical returns of the market have been ten percent. The market over long periods is fairly predictable. Any thirty- to forty-year slice of the market's history will closely match the long-term average. Only short periods will demonstrate unpredictability and heightened risk. This is not a concern for a long-term investor who understands that the dips are temporary, and the market always grows over time.

Diversification in your investment portfolio is what will protect you from the risk that individual stocks or sectors can produce over short periods. The buy-and-hold strategy is by far the best option for long-term wealth creation. Engaging in trading activities costs more in fees, and it has been demonstrated to be a less effective way of investing not just for beginners, but professionals as well.

In Practice

In terms of traditional investing, stocks historically have provided the best returns. However, many good-quality stocks can be expensive to buy. Using ETFs, REITs, and index funds is a low-cost way of diversifying your investment over many stocks. They will match the performance of a sector or market, which is just what you need. You have been provided with practical examples of how an aggressive, balanced, and defensive portfolio is diversified. Young people should be using a more aggressive fund for most of their working lives, changing to a more balanced fund closer to retirement. People getting into investing much later in life should play it safe and use a balanced approach. Likewise, the balanced portfolio would be best for shorter goals, such as a mortgage down payment. After retirement, the defensive portfolio would make better sense when you have made your wealth and simply want to preserve it.

If your employer offers a 401(k) or 403(b), then it must be your first priority. If you are offered an employer match, then all the better. Try your best to contribute enough to earn the maximum employer contribution. Your work retirement plan will offer the highest amount of money that you can invest in a tax-protected vehicle. IRAs are useful as a secondary investment channel, and if they are your only option, then contribute the maximum. Roth and traditional accounts have their benefits. To reduce your after-retirement tax obligations, choose your account wisely. If your retirement income will exceed your working salary, then a Roth is generally the recommended choice. Do not forget that, if the investment bug has bitten you, then getting a deduction on your traditional contributions can be invested as well. This could leave you in a better after- tax position compared to the Roth setup.

As far as accounts go, you have many good options. The fees and commissions that you pay are your main consideration. Directing your own account or selecting a robo-advisor or mutual fund are all perfectly acceptable choices. Neither is better than the other. Your account must match your needs for diversification and average returns. Being more comfortable with a managed account is just fine. Having a monthly automatic transfer is the key.

Old school wisdom states that you should always pay off debt first. This can create a situation that delays investment indefinitely. Certainly, keep your debt to a minimum, and pay it off as fast as you can, but not at the expense of investing. Particularly if you are young, the lifetime returns on a diversified aggressive portfolio should offer higher interest than your mortgage or student loan debt.

Good investors stick with their goals and don't panic with every rumor that they hear about the market or a sector. Be realistic; the magic of compound interest takes time to get rolling. You will not become a millionaire overnight, and you should not pick your stocks with that expectation in mind. Patience is a virtue.

It Starts Yesterday

You have been given basic exposure to more complex investment options, such as derivatives, that require a margin account. Derivatives, cryptocurrency, and commodities trading are nothing to be afraid of, but they are areas that necessitate a great deal of knowledge and continuous learning. My best advice would be to avoid using your retirement contributions for this type of investing. It can be an enjoyable side-venture with spare cash, but your core goals are more safely served by the traditional approach of buying and holding.

Direct real estate investment methods are more accessible these days. They too require additional research and investigation. You have the principles though, which are also applicable when choosing your own home. You now know more about buying a home that will also be a genuine investment.

You now have the essential toolkit to grow your wealth and to take charge of your personal financial future. Successful investors that retire in peace and comfort are everyday people like you and me. They simply have habits that ensure their success. You will be one of them because you know what they know. There is no more fear, just a need for action. Start now and thank yourself later. If there is one message that stays with you years after putting this book down, it is this: Know how much money you need to be happy for over twenty years of retirement. Know how much you need to invest every month to achieve that with a realistic return. Stick with that goal, and never stray. If this is all that you remember, then your investment journey will have a happy ending. Get going! Time is of the essence.

Special Bonus!

Want this Bonus Book for Free?

Get **FREE**, unlimited access to it and to all of my new books by joining the Fan Base!

SCAN WITH YOUR CAMERA **TO JOIN!**

References

Carey, T.W. (2021, February 1). Best Online Stock Brokers for Beginners. Investopedia, www.investopedia.com/best-brokers-for-beginners-4587873.

Chen, J. (2020, March 16). Exchange-Traded Fund (ETF). Investopedia. https://www.investopedia.com/terms/e/etf.asp

Chen, J. (2021, March 26). Sector Breakdown. Investopedia. https://www.investopedia.com/terms/s/sector-breakdown.asp

Derivatives - Overview, Types, Advantages and Disadvantages. (2019). Corporate Finance Institute. https://corporatefinanceinstitute.com/resources/knowledge/trading-investing/derivatives/

Fabozzi, F.J. (2004). Fixed Income Analysis. CFA Institute

Jackson, A.-L. (2020, November 12). What Is Forex Trading? Forbes Advisor. https://www.forbes.com/advisor/investing/what-is-forex-trading/

Maranjian, S. (2020, February 2). The Janitor Who Became A Multi-Millionaire by Retirement. The Motley Fool. https://www.fool.com/retirement/2020/02/02/the-janitor-who-became-a-multi-millionaire-by-reti.aspx

Maritz, N.G. (1993). The Property Business: Readings in Real Estate. Unisa Press.

Marx, J. (2003). Investment Management. Van Schaik.

Middleton, J. (2004). Detox your finances. Infinite Ideas Company.

Mohr, P. (2000). Economic indicators. Unisa Press.

Norris, E. (2021, January 28). Cash Account vs. Margin Account: What Is the Difference? Investopedia. https://www.investopedia.com/ask/answers/100314/whats-difference-between-cash-account-and-margin-account.asp#:~:text=Key%20Takeaways-

Retirement Presentation CFP Board. (2019). The Morning Consult https://www.cfp.net/-/media/images/cfp-board/cfp-board-images/reports-and-publications/cfp-board-morning-consult-retirementpreparednesssurvey-2019.pdf?la=en&hash=ECC8C62E12723B392647015C2FB76908

Retirement Topics - IRA Contribution Limits. (2020, December 15) Internal Revenue Service. www.irs.gov/retirement-plans/plan-participant-employee/retirement-topics-ira-contribution-limits#:~:text=For%202021%2C%202020%20and%202019.

Rich, B. (2016, February 29). Warren Buffett Explains Why Over Time Stocks Go Up. Forbes. https://www.forbes.com/sites/bryanrich/2016/02/29/warren-buffett-explains-why-over-time-stocks-go-up/

Royal, J. (2021, April 22). What Is Cryptocurrency? Beginners Guide to Digital Cash. NerdWallet. https://www.nerdwallet.com/article/investing/cryptocurrency-7-things-to-know

Schwab-Pomerantz, C. (2020, July 16). Roth vs. Traditional 401(k)—Which Is Better? Schwab Brokerage. https://www.schwab.com/resource-center/insights/content/roth-vs-traditional-401-k-which-is-better#:~:text=The%20basic%20difference%20between%20a

Vincent, E. (2020, July 16). Top 7 Reasons to Start Investing Early. - Tradingsim. https://tradingsim.com/blog/top-7-reasons-to-start-investing-early/

www.ingramcontent.com/pod-product-compliance
Lightning Source LLC
Chambersburg PA
CBHW070802220526
45466CB00002B/509